Horatio Willis Dresser

Methods and Problems of Spiritual Healing

Horatio Willis Dresser

Methods and Problems of Spiritual Healing

ISBN/EAN: 9783337334673

Printed in Europe, USA, Canada, Australia, Japan

Cover: Foto ©Lupo / pixelio.de

More available books at **www.hansebooks.com**

METHODS AND PROBLEMS OF SPIRITUAL HEALING

BY

HORATIO W. DRESSER

Author of "The Power of Silence," "The Perfect Whole,"
"In Search of a Soul," "Voices of Hope"

G. P. PUTNAM'S SONS
NEW YORK AND LONDON
The Knickerbocker Press
1899

COPYRIGHT, 1899
BY
HORATIO W. DRESSER

The Knickerbocker Press, New York

PREFACE.

The author is not in the practice of mental healing, nor does he deem himself competent to give advice concerning specific application of the mental cure. He is not a follower of any sect, and does not subscribe to the full creed of those who advocate mental remedies in the cure of disease. He is simply a truth-seeker; and the following pages contain the results of fifteen years of observation, during which it has been his privilege to witness the successful application of the principles he advocates. The purpose of the book is quite as much to stimulate thought as to offer practical suggestions; for the entire subject is still in its infancy, and the greatest good the author can hope to accomplish is to promote investigation.

H. W. D.

BOSTON, *February, 1899.*

I.

"He who is made alive in heart is whole."

THE subject of healing is in many respects the most difficult question with which the student of spiritual thought has to deal, since there is such wide diversity of opinion in regard to it, and because in its higher aspects the experience itself is in large part indescribable. There is much that cannot be told, and much that would be of little value even if it could be put into words, for the reason that each must perceive its reality through individual experience in order to know what it means. Nearly all the problems of life are, in fact, involved in this question. The whole subject is so complicated, and in a sense still so obscure, that one is at a loss where to begin, what to regard as accepted fact, and what to reject as mere theory.

Glowing accounts of cures by the mental method may be had in abundance; and there are thousands who are ready to give evidence that they have been not only entirely healed, but permanently converted to the philosophy of mental healing. But the simple facts, shorn of personal bias and stated in scientific language, are not so readily obtainable. Yet, as the same difficulties are in large part encountered whenever one seeks fundamental truth, one may as well make the effort here as elsewhere. I shall therefore treat the subject in a general, often in a sceptical and somewhat superficial way, approaching the real problem by degrees, and suggesting meanwhile some of the secondary questions which the central problem itself presents.

But first let me confess the sense of wonder which attaches to the entire process even after one has made it the study of years. The subject is, in fact, very much like that of any specific attempt to wrest from the universe every detail of one of its secrets: something always escapes us. When Nature wakes from her long winter's sleep, and vegetation expands and grows in the light of the warm summer's sun, what causes this marvellous change? Can anybody tell? The scientific man may enumerate the steps whereby the great transformation takes place, just as he may analyze the physical basis of life. But what is the dormant *life* itself, what is the hidden force without which the nicely adapted substances are mere collections of chemicals? Apparently, we know a great deal about every factor except the one which somehow animates and uses them all.

Likewise with the phenomena of healing. One may easily describe the general conditions of healing, the experience of becoming open to spiritual power, of directing this power to the patient through concentration or suggestion, as well as the physiological process accompanying the mental change. But are we not a bit hasty when, neglecting the real point at issue, we confidently affirm that one factor in particular has wrought the cure? This favorite factor of ours,— faith, auto-suggestion, telepathy, the prayer of silence, or what not, — like a drug heralded as a great specific, may have been but the last in a long chain of helpful causes which played only the culminating part. Or the case might have been like that mentioned by Dr. Hillis, of Chicago, in a recent sermon on healing : —

In Iowa a gentleman at whose home a reception was given, wheeled out to the porch the chair of his mother, who had not taken a step for many years. During the gayeties of the evening a hanging lamp fell with a crash to the floor. When the flames had been subdued and quiet restored, the mother was found standing in the room, having lost her rheumatism and her pain. Years before nature had cured the ailment, but the woman waited for some event or person to rouse the dormant will. Had some scientist or faith healer or theosophist happened along, a cure almost miraculous would have lent the healer great fame.

Obviously, the matter of credit must be set aside; for at best the physician is only an instrument of the healing power. "We amuse the patient, while Nature heals the disease," said the wise French physician, speaking for his profession.

Admittedly, every slightest circumstance, the entire state at the time, is involved; and, in order to return a full answer to the question, one must consider the nature of mind, the constitution of matter, the nature of pleasure and pain, of health and disease, the ultimate meaning of suffering, and the experiences of healers of different schools.

Let us, then, consider a number of specific cases, and examine them as much in detail as possible, in order to tabulate the various factors; for the day is past when one may safely generalize about mental healing, or even about disease. Diseases can no more be classed under one head as "errors of the mind" than as physical entities, or under the terms of some compromise between these extremes. A man's trouble may have as little foundation as the suggestions which caused the death of the English criminal, in the instance so often referred to; and it may be cured by a simple suggestion. His entire nature, his whole complaining, nervous, or apprehensive habit of thought may be involved, so that nothing less than a complete change of living will suffice, in which case he must be gradually taught to see that he creates his own misery. Or the trouble may be so largely physical that mere enlightenment would never cure him. In most cases of mental cure the doctor is inclined to doubt if there really was a disease, and in the same way the mental healers stand by each other in opposition to medical practice.

According to some, disease comes from germs: others deem it the result of obsession. Some will tell you that all diseases come from troubles of the stomach; in other words, indigestion and insufficient mastication. Others trace all disease to excessive bodily heat. Some diseases, like typhoid fever, apparently have to run their course, even under mental treatment, although their course may be greatly hastened. An easily influenced person may be cured of a dread disease far more readily than an obstinate one can be relieved of some slight malady. Only daughters and wealthy ladies who board prove difficult patients, while those who have no time or money to be ill are scarcely in need of a physician. A credulous person is an easy subject for mental treatment; while the highly cultivated intellect deems the therapeutic suggestions absurd, and is therefore slow to respond. The disease of a baby may come entirely from its mother, who must be healed before the child can be cured. And so on through a long list of interesting facts, all pointing to the conclusion that few cases are alike, while in most instances neither the disease nor its cure is to be described apart from the temperament of the individual.

But let us take a typical case, and consider the

factors of cure in the patient. The sufferer is troubled by a malady which originated in fear, nervous shock, suppressed emotion, accident, haunting mental pictures, or some other cause which threw mind and body out of harmony. The first trouble was probably of slight consequence, and might have been either mental or physical or both, but through misunderstanding of the sensation of pain, and by wrong treatment, it has now been magnified into a disturbance which the medical doctors cannot cure, and which the patient fears may lead to fatal disease.

For usually those who try the mental cure turn to it as a last resort. They have lost faith in drugs, and this is a decided gain. They are uncertain about the new method, but are willing to try it. This is also favorable, for where there is receptivity the healer's task is much the easier. Some, indeed, experiment with mental healing to please their friends. But it is better, on the whole, that the patient have faith, that he be personally eager to give the new cure a fair trial. Occasionally, it is true, people have been cured of drunkenness and other habits by members of the family who treated them unbeknown. Still, if there be not conscious willingness to be helped, there must at least be sympathy, affinity, subconscious openness of some sort; and usually there is unconscious co-operation.

Receptivity, then, we may note as one of the factors instrumental in effecting a cure. The patient's disposition, as we have seen, is another factor; for people vary, from those who are naturally so rigid that they will not yield any condition till forced to relax, to those who are so pliable that one must avoid bringing too much power to bear at a time. Receptivity is, therefore, a variable factor, and is closely connected with the degree of emotion; coldness of intellect and non-receptivity being found together.

Auto-suggestion in the form of expectant attention is another noteworthy factor. The mental healer requests the patient to assume a comfortable physical attitude, and "become as receptive as possible." This self-induced attitude is somewhat analogous to hypnosis, which is defined by Dr. H. A. Parkyn as "a state of mental quiescence in which the suggestion of the operator has an exaggerated effect upon the mind of the subject." In such a state, even the absurd affirmations and negations, "You have no headache," "You have no head," are as effective as gospel truth, *if the mind accepts them;* for the desideratum is to make an *impression* upon the mind consciously or subconsciously. When the patient is suffering from acute pain or fears some "uncanny" result, the auto-suggestion is, of course, unfavorable. In such cases, and in instances of "real" disease, the cure must be wrought almost wholly by the healer, frequently amidst the opposition and countersuggestions of relatives, friends, and the family physician, who has given up the case as "hopeless." Here, again, it is impossible to generalize.

Yet in many cases the *desire* to be healed has so much to do with the cure, the expectancy of relief, and the effort to help one's self by looking away from the trouble, that it is well always for the patient to follow the directions of the healer as faithfully as possible. Occasionally the patient's faith is sufficient to accomplish a large part of the work. Sometimes a former patient will write for absent help, and the healer will forget the appointment. But so familiar is the patient with the general requirements that the right conditions will be observed almost unconsciously, and relief will come without the aid of any factor but this faith and receptivity.

I have known of former patients who asked the privilege of coming occasionally to sit in the chair where they had once received treatment, as they found it easier to lay off their burdens and become receptive. It is probable that, if we could assume the attitude of complete receptivity to the healing power, if we could become as a little child, this would be sufficient to produce the cure. The animal who has been injured and lies down quietly until Nature heals the hurt illustrates this receptivity. Wonderful cures are wrought among the ignorant and superstitious simply because they have not the doubts which put barriers in the way of the healing power.

Here, then, is an aspect of the subject which it is well to bear constantly in mind. Frequently the whole matter is in the patient's hands; and it is possible to help one's self on any occasion if one will remove the obstacles to Nature's resident restorative power,— the fear, doubt, anxiety, tension, all states of mind tending to draw one into self, to shut in and contract where one should open out and expand. Even in cases of chronic invalidism, where, for example, the person has been unable to walk and is gradually restored to health through the agency of a healer, there is often little apparent change until the person is *convinced* of the cure and is willing to make conscious effort. It might therefore be stated as a general law that the patient stands in need of the healer only to the degree that he either fails to help or is temporarily incapable of relying upon himself. Yet one should avoid the erroneous conclusion which some have reached,— namely, that the whole process is subjective,— for in most cases the essential impulse is given by another mind.

> "Why should we shrink where nature never shrinks?
> Why should we not take heart of her whose heart
> Enfolds the germ of all things,— dare to stand
> With spirits bared before the ineffable light,
> As she against the glory of the dawn
> Lifts naked arms, all-welcoming the day?"

II.

WHEN we have given credit to the factors of cure in the patient,— desire to be healed, faith, temperament, receptivity, auto-suggestion, expectant attention, and the rest,— what shall we say of those cases in which all this proved insufficient, and the patient was cured by a mental healer? Let us return to our typical case; namely, the person who, receptive and willing, but unable to help himself, comes for silent treatment. What are the factors on the healer's side?

In the first place there is desire to heal, sympathy, a longing to play one's part in Nature's wonderful process. The healer has himself suffered, found relief by mental means, and knows what it is to be freed from bondage to fear, medicine, and doctors. He is not a believer in disease as something that is likely to seize a person externally. He believes that suffering is neither an affliction nor a necessity, but a condition brought about through ignorance, wrong ways of living and thinking; that one may learn to take life so as to avoid sickness altogether, finally overcoming all friction, so that an experience which would once have seemed a curse shall now prove a blessing by the way in which it is received; in short, that our understanding or mental attitude is of more consequence in our reaction upon life than any and all of its material conditions. Accordingly, his first effort is to change the mental attitude of the patient.

This may often be effected by audible explanation; as, for example, when the patient is uncharitable or is suffering from suppressed grief, one can in a few quiet words indicate the wiser way. But we will assume that the average patient of whom we are speaking really requires the silent help. The patient comes in the willing attitude before described. The healer is in a sympathetic state. If intuitive, he does not ask questions of the patient, and will not permit a rehearsal of symptoms and sufferings; for this will tend to refresh the troubles, fears, and mental pictures. The past is passed, and the patient should now be concerned solely with the ideal future. The healer sits by the patient, and asks him to become quiet and receptive. The patient is not to force himself to be still, but become restfully expectant, and to think rather of the healer than of himself.

The healer thereupon turns the mind aside from the noisy world without, excludes sound, light, and physical feeling as much as possible, and rises to the kingdom of the inner self, or soul,—just as one might ascend a mountain summit in order to survey the world from a higher region. As a rule, people find it difficult to concentrate and withdraw the attention from the outer world, because many thoughts rush in upon the mind. But after a time it becomes almost instinctive to focus the attention on that Power which, always with the soul, only need be recognized in order to come actively uppermost in consciousness. Any uplifting thought that will enable one to realize the omnipresence of love, wisdom, goodness, power, will bring about the result, and it is best not to commit one's self to a set form of words; nor should one approach any two cases alike, but seek the wisdom which applies to a particular case. Yet oftentimes the same realization, such as, "In him we live and move and have our being," is the most helpful thought when entering the silence; and frequently one uses the same words or suggestions with which to command one's self and quiet the troubled atmosphere of the patient,—namely, "Peace, be still, peace, peace!"

There is, however, in the more spiritual process no reasoning, no attempt to transfer definite thoughts, and *no effort to control or hypnotize the mind of the patient.* It is rather the healer's place to bring down a gentle, soothing atmosphere about the patient, from which the latter shall absorb according to his need and receptivity. The spiritual healer is not himself the all-powerful mind or factor: he is the willing instrument of the higher

Power. His desire is to become spiritually open and free: then to induce the same state in the patient.

If, therefore, one uses certain ideal suggestions or passages of Scripture, in order to hold the thought in the right direction, it should be remembered that the words are only stepping-stones to the higher plane. It is not the word or thought that is the reality: it is the living essence which the word or thought suggests. That essence, or Spirit, is ever with us. God is here within, inseparable from the soul; and, when the soul feels the divine presence, it possesses the thing itself, and has little need of words. To realize this oneness with Deity, and withdraw the consciousness from all that is painful and morbid, is the substance of the silent spiritual method.

The first step, let me repeat, is to direct the consciousness toward the omnipresent Spirit, to become peaceful, quiet, poised, *master of the situation*. When one is thus open and free, one may turn to the sufferer, and in the same gentle yet strong and stimulating spirit, envelope him with an atmosphere so powerful that no inharmonious condition either of mind or body can long withstand it. It is a well-established fact that the power thus directed toward the patient meets resistance where the sufferer is in discord,— that is, mind and body are open, free, responsive, except in particular regions; and here the healing power meets an obstacle. Nature is trying to restore equilibrium, and meets opposition at this restricted point. Even if one knows nothing about the patient's trouble at the outset, the healing experience will soon reveal the location of it, because one's thought directed toward the patient will meet this obstruction, the healing power will bear down upon it, until gradually the condition begins to change in somewhat the same way that ice melts under the heat of the sun. The thought of the healer directs and focuses the power where it is most needed, and holds it there persistently, with the idea that the condition is gradually changing, that the patient is giving up his fears, haunting mental pictures, and painful consciousness of sensation, and becoming open to the higher Power. This is continued until an impression is made, until enough has been accomplished to start the right reaction; then the change continues subconsciously, even after the treatment is finished.

The healer is like the person with good sight who offers kindly assistance to a blind man. The one with good sight sees the way open before him as he proceeds, and therefore steps along confidently. In this spirit of confidence one should guide the sufferer, because one knows the way, because of what one knows about the human mind, the effect of thought, the nature of disease, and the rich possibilities of our spiritual existence. One should not dwell upon symptoms and doubts, but see the *outcome*, think of the patient as *he ought to be*, in good health, poised, calm, and strong. One should be stronger in the right thought than the sufferer is in the wrong, penetrating persistently to the very core of the disturbance, opening and expanding it, until the new life is started with a thrill throughout mind and body.

III.

Here the question arises, Does the healer really open the mind to an outside force which is then directed toward the patient, or is this force resident in the healer? Or, assuming that there is a definite suggestion given or a thought transferred to the patient, does this thought merely quicken the dormant healing power in the patient? Probably many healers would maintain that power or life is actually absorbed from without by the healer, and also in the process of self-help. At any rate, a state of mind is aroused of which it is desirable that the patient receive the subconscious benefit. Whether there be definite thought transference or simply the consciousness of concentrating power toward the patient, the result is evidently the same; that is, the thought probably does not travel. It is the motion or vibration which is transferred, obviously through a substance finer than the ether, in which our minds are bathed. And, if the healing power is omnipresent, there is no question of outside and inside, the essential being the establishment of a centre of activity for that power in the patient.

We may then consider the healing power as

potentially resident in both healer and patient. It may even be in a state of tension in the patient,— the natural tendency of the organism to right itself,— the pain being a sign that this tendency is interfered with by wrong treatment, fear, nervousness, the effort to draw in and bear the pain. The mental treatment removes this opposition, and co-operates with Nature by giving the mind a healthier direction, and hastening the activity of the healing power.

It is essential to remember that there is a soul or higher nature craving expression, a latent ideal toward which our forces are persistently striving. If the patient is unaware of this evolutionary process, this tendency toward the perfect, the power is resisted and confined, and suffering results. If one is undeveloped on the affectional side of one's nature, if the intellect is uncultivated, or if one is in need of physical exercise, this undeveloped or one-sided region is the seat of creative activity. Nature is striving through us to realize a type, to actualize a rounded ideal. She is irresistibly persistent in this endeavor; and, if she cannot make an impression upon us by gentle means, she must resort to something vigorous or painful. There is a sort of natural rhythm of development. Those who are well developed and wise move with it. Those who are unfinished in any particular meet it with resistance. The effort, therefore, both in helping another and in self-help, should be to co-operate with this natural process. This may be done by trying to picture the ideal.

One cannot accomplish much at a time. One should select one tendency after another, master it, and be content with moderate growth. It is the straining after ideals which is the bane of many sensitive minds. But it is not so much growth that we need as realization. Therefore there is no means of self-help more effectual than to settle quietly into the living present. It may be assumed in every case of illness and of pain that there is tension of some sort, a reaching out toward the future in fear or anxiety, a too eager desire to accomplish. There is worriment over financial matters or nervous resignation to endure pain. We are constantly wishing that some one might come or that something might happen, and this constant discontent causes an equally constant waste of energy. If this strain can be removed, the resistance to Nature's forces will cease.

Put yourself entirely in the present, trustfully, restfully, calmly. You are an immortal soul, and have all eternity before you. Time is of no real consequence: it is simply a matter of mathematical convenience. Space, too, has little meaning for the soul. There is no place in the wide universe where there is more wisdom and power than here in this living present. The omniscient God is here, the source of all life and goodness. He is unlimited by space, unhampered by time. You are eternally a part of him and of his life. You stand individually for some aspect of wisdom and power which no other soul can represent as well. Your experience is a progressive awakening to the consciousness of that Power, and with the discovery of greater power comes greater ability to express it. Peace, then. Trust, and be receptive to that Power. Do not nervously strive to grow, but let the soul expand. Let Nature and the subconscious mind do their utmost for you, while you devote your conscious thought to realization of the divine presence, to ways and means of making that presence known among your fellow-men.

Nothing is more fundamental, more effectual, than such an act of will or concentrated attention. Let the outer universe be as real as it may, let the disease be a physical malady, if you will, the fact remains that all this is known only through consciousness, that we are really living a life of mind, and that it is the will which is the active cause or directive force. The life force is consciousness. It is consciousness fixed in a given direction which enables us to form habits, to learn an art or science. It is consciousness misled and misdirected which has built the disease from which we wish to be free, and consciousness must undo what it has done by seeking a new and healthier direction.

This shifting of attention is very much the same in its effect as though one were to turn the body squarely around and walk in the opposite direction. The act of will is slight which causes the change, but it carries the whole activity of the being with it. Or it is like an absorbing story or play which holds the attention so that one forgets time, place, and all else; the difference being this,— that by choosing the thought of oneness with God and eternity you may make the changed state of mind permanent by opening the mind and receiving new life and power directly from the fountain-head. The thought of oneness with God, the realization of the rounded ideal, broadens the consciousness, lifts one to a wider realm; and this is needed above all else. For probably in all cases of illness there is a contraction in some part of the body, either in brain and nerves or in nerves and muscles. The atoms are drawn too closely together, and there must be expansion of body. This results from the elevation of thought to the plane of spiritual consciousness. It throws the atoms apart, the confined power has a chance to come forth, the nervous tension is removed; and gradually, as the mind becomes peaceful and happy, the entire physical system is freed, in much the same way whereby one is warmed on a cold day by going into the sunlight.

But how does this realization of the divine ideal, and of oneness with God through spiritual concentration, reach another person and cause similar expansion? Probably the best illustration of this process is that of the transfer of sound vibration. When two pianos are in adjoining rooms, if a note is struck on one, the corresponding chord on the other will vibrate.* Likewise in human speech. The will or desire on my part to communicate with you causes my ideas to take shape in language which you understand, a process is set up in my brain, transmitted to the vocal chords, and thus by vibration to your ear, brain, and finally to your consciousness. And your understanding of what I say is precisely dependent on the attention which you give to it, the receptivity to it, and the sympathy of experience. If you have entered the silence and communed with God, you know what I mean. If not, my words convey little or nothing to you: it is the experience or consciousness which avails.

In the healing process the communication is very much simplified, although still of a vibratory character. You are receptive, and need help; and I desire to help you. We sit together, and enter into sympathy mentally. I do not try to force my thought upon you, but you give me your attention. The sympathy between us has annihilated space;

---

* For this illustration, I am indebted to Casey, "The Problem Restated."

and, as I turn aside from the outer world and rise to the plane of soul silence or divine communion, your mind consciously or subconsciously receives the benefit of my realization, through this sympathetic receptivity. You may feel nothing at the time, but a seed has been sown in the subconscious mind where it will germinate and grow. In other words, physically speaking, work has been done: the healing power has been directed to the contracted or tense centre, the particles have been driven farther apart; and this expansion brought about at the inmost centre is sure to result sooner or later in a change of which you will be duly conscious.

There is much that is still mysterious in this process. But the essential, for the healer, is to remember that mind is fundamental, that probably matter itself is ultimately psychic or conscious. It is not always necessary even to blot out mental pictures,* nor reason away whims and fears. Sometimes, it is true, if one fairly faces a fear, it may be easily mastered. There is a saying among the Sandwich Islanders, that the warrior gains the power of every foe he conquers. But it is not well to fight one's mental states, but to turn positively away from them. See the better mental pictures of yourself as you ought to be, and these will efface the old.

* The relation of mental pictures to the cause and cure of disease has been ably discussed by L. E. Whipple, "The Philosophy of Mental Healing," New York, the Metaphysical Publishing Company.

The keynote to the entire process is to strike a new chord, to change the attention or will. It is, in fine, a question of placing our allegiance. Shall we live in the consciousness of sensation, of self, in memory of the past, in trouble, fear, worriment, in matter and circumstance? Or shall we dwell upon the end to be reached through all this process, the larger self, the spirit, **the real** or eternal? Shall we seek the kingdom of heaven, that all else may come, or seek first *things*, hoping that the kingdom may be added? The mind is limited in power, and must choose*; for there is literally no room both for trouble and for trust. Either I am to look upon myself as all-important, and try to have things circulate about *me*, or I am to regard the infinite as first and myself as a part of it. To lose self, that one may find it, is, in fact, the essence of healing; for, invariably, there is too great consciousness of self whenever there is illness and trouble.

* For an able discussion of the changing phenomena of consciousness, see "The Principles of Psychology," Professor James, vol. i., chap. x.

IV.

TRUE healing, therefore, means to trust God more, to love more, to become at peace, to get out of self, to understand self. It comes by laying fear aside, through aspiration, by becoming adjusted to the body and to one's environment. It is not mere personal influence: it is helpfulness, it is love, it is sacred. It is not the giving of one's own strength and health. It does not exhaust. It is mutually helpful and renewing to healer and patient.

It is helpful for a group of people to sit in the silence, as though one should say to the rest: Peace, let us be still within, and commune with that Presence of which all life is a sharing, to which all conduct should be a helpful witness. Whatever calamity may come to us in the future, let it come when it must; for it were better that we should not foreknow it. Each of you will probably go away from here when our silence is broken; but at present why not lose all sense of time until the hour has come? This bit of existence is infinitely small and trivial; but in some way it fits into the great universe, and unites us with all that lives. Eternity is here as surely as anywhere or in any time. Life is a great unbroken whole; and from the centre of each consciousness, as if it were the heart of being, vibrations of thought and love extend to the uttermost confines of the whole. Each of us exists within, and yet is not identical with the Spirit, so that for each he is personally the Father. For each he has provided in that wonderful way of perfect wisdom which establishes the limit, sees the end, implants the ideal, yet leaves freedom for all to think and have experience, freedom to sin, until at last in the fulness of time we shall awaken from ignorance, learn the wisdom of experience, and choose the life of devotion to the highest.

From this present trouble of ours there is a way of escape. Self alone stands in the way. Yet even this is no ground for complaint. If we are rightly adjusted to the creative rhythm or process, we shall not be troubled by it longer than is necessary to teach us its lesson. Then let us be content. Let us drop fear and impatience, in quiet trust and restfulness. Peace, be still! There is nothing to fear. Nothing can come to us without receptivity or willingness on our part. We therefore hold the keys to our minds. We can accomplish anything through faith, with sufficient time.

We are not responsible for the universe, nor for the lives of any of its people. We cannot fully explain our belief in the goodness of things; but the belief is there, and the only fault seems to be that we do not trust more. We cannot tell fully why we believe in God. It may seem audacious even to speak of him as though we had penetrated life's secret far enough to describe our oneness with him. But here again we apparently err only because we do not live more in the thought of him. This deep, fundamental basis of life is the permanent substance, or being, which goes forth as the word, or spirit, and expresses itself through all the changes of form, of space and time.

This present, passing experience, life as you and I live it, is such a going forth, partaking of the living essence of God. It does not proceed at random, but is directed by perfect wisdom and love. Every part is adjusted to every other part, and all parts are governed by the one central purpose which makes the universe a realm of law and order. That which guides and inspires is sufficient for all needs. There is no opposing power to break and mar the creative process. All is steady march. No fact, no experience, no thought, lies outside the whole. In each fact, each thought, the whole is reproduced in miniature. One need not travel to find the whole. Space and time add no new principles. But everywhere, in ever-changing forms and in ever-fresh experience, the one law, the one life, the one spirit, or wisdom, is again and again reproduced.

Therefore in the work of healing there is one central question : What is the universal will seeking to accomplish in this particular phase of your life or the patient's life? How is that tendency opposed? Where is the friction located? What may be done to remove it ? *

In addition to such realizations as the above, and the methods already described, it is sometimes helpful to isolate the troublesome thought or disturbed portion of the body by assuming an attitude of quiet indifference to it. If the fear of some possible calamity comes into mind, it will not be developed into an absorbing mental state unless one permits the intellect to be controlled by it. Therefore say to this part of yourself, " Anticipate and worry, if you will: meantime I will enjoy myself." If you are restless at night, say to yourself : "Toss about and think as long as you choose. When you have finished, I will go to sleep." Or, if your brain is over-active in one direction, when you wish to think about something else, say, "Grind away : I am content to await in serenity." Nine times out of ten the relief is immediate, for the mind does not care to think when one is so agreeable. It is overcome with kindness, or, more truly, the seat of power has been shifted elsewhere. In the same way one may overcome ner-

---

* Those who prefer specific application of the mental healing principle will find such a series of specific affirmations in "The Breath of Life," by Ursula N. Gestefeld, New York, The Gestefeld Publishing Company.

vous intensity by this flank movement. Start a centre of calmness and poise somewhere else, and say, "Serene, I fold my hands and wait." If you are willing, good nature will accomplish what resistance could not.

An important point to remember in connection with the rapid inner changes experienced by sensitive minds, while under silent treatment, is the fact that the sensation is very much exaggerated. One is inclined to give way to fear, and, momentarily at least, to doubt the whole process of spiritual help. But, when one learns what it is that is at work, all fear seems absurd; for Nature will not desert us half-way. One cannot safely judge by sensation. In finely organized natures the sensations are so acute that one would be entirely misled by them. Pain, when thus read, is not an accurate record of truth. It is overdrawn, and, rightly understood, should not cause fear, but its opposite, trust.

A sure method of rising above sensation, or getting out of self-consciousness, when one is too subjective, is to turn the attention gradually, until one is at length entirely absorbed by objects in the outside world. Pick out one detail after another in the scene before you, until thought by thought you slowly emerge into the world about you, and have no room left for the imprisoning consciousness of self.

Probably the most effective way to overcome the tendency to wander away from this present existence, to become partially disconnected from the body or project one's self at a distance, is to settle down into the physical body with real joy in the beautiful world of earth life. One should take regular physical exercise, and put the mind upon each bodily movement. It is helpful, too, to feel one's self alive in all parts of the body, to think down into the feet and become poised there. For always, when one is in a normal condition, one is very much at home in the body; and mind and body are mutually adjusted.

The clew to the entire process of healing is the concentration of thought upon some other centre or plane of consciousness, that the resident recuperative power may enjoy an unrestricted field of activity, in every way aided, not in the least hindered, by your thought. If your powers of concentration are such that you can entirely detach your consciousness from the thought of disease, the sensation of pain, and carry it over to the soul, or spiritual side of life, so much the better. For the desideratum is to lift the entire process to the spiritual plane, to live in thought with the ideal, to regard mind and body rather from the point of view of the soul than to look upon the soul from the standpoint of the body. To live more with God, this it is spiritually to heal and be healed. To aspire, to hope, to love, to co-operate with God. For healing is loving and renewing: it is a part of the great creative work of the universe.

V.

To what extent is it advisable to give and receive mental treatment? Evidently, so far only as the recipient is unable to practise self-healing, only when the healer believes it right, and in cases where the patient feels prompted to become receptive. For spiritual healing should be guided by the principle of spiritual affinity, and by the love motive, never by the desire to make money. It should be undertaken when one believes that one can be helpful, not for experimental reasons only. One should not in any case promise a cure, nor ought one to assume the responsibility of critical illness. In cases where death may result, and mental treatment is found helpful, but not all-powerful, it is wiser to leave the responsibility with the regular physician.

Since the mental cure is still in an experimental stage, and is not yet legally recognized, it is wise to keep well within the limits of the law. Christian Scientists * who have permitted people to die rather than call upon a regular physician, have harmed the cause of mental healing more than they have helped it by their fanatical zeal. The time is yet

* The author wishes it distinctly understood that he does not in any way subscribe to the creed of the Christian Scientists.

to come when the mental cure shall be given its place side by side with conventional methods of cure. Even then it may not wholly displant its predecessors. There is a great field for its application in connection with physical remedies. Whether it will ever become the sole method of cure, time alone can tell, since time alone can reveal its limitations and further possibilities. It is true, many already claim that it has healed disease in all its forms; and marvellous stories are current of sudden cures, the healing, and even the replacing, of broken bones. But the majority will believe such cures possible only when they have personal knowledge of them; and the accurate in statement know that even the best healers sometimes fail to reach severe cases, such as blindness and deafness, where physiological difficulties have proved too great for mental power to overcome.

Furthermore, the ideal healer has yet to be evolved; for the theory has advanced far more rapidly than the practice. At its best, the healer's work is a life of self-denying service; and there are not many who are ready to undergo all that is required to heal invalids of an exquisitely sensitive type. The practice of silent treatment tends to make the healer exceedingly sympathetic and sensitive, and it is sometimes very difficult to throw off the mental atmospheres of patients. More than once I have heard healers of the sensitive type say of this kind of work, "It is all wrong," meaning of course that to enter so far into the conditions of another, to perceive the diseased states of poisoned or tobacco-laden tissues, and to bear another's burden, is too much for any one to do for another. For those who have such insight and sympathy as this the wiser rule would seem to be that it is greater love to withhold than to give, since one is not called upon to work out another's salvation, but simply to indicate the way. Whenever there is contamination or mixture of mental atmospheres, one has not yet attained the state of development required for the most healthful work as a mental healer. Such conditions imply that the healer is not yet sound, not yet sufficiently positive and strong in himself.

However, one should not be too severe in criticising those who cannot keep free from the aches and pains of their patients. A large majority of mental healers were formerly invalids, who began to help others before they were themselves fully restored to health. It is through such experiences in the struggle for health that these people have acquired their wisdom. Actual acquaintance with sorrow and suffering gives sympathy which no theory could supplant. They know who have lived, not they who merely have thought. Some healers have suffered more than the most sorely afflicted of their patients; yet this rich experience has given them the power to help, which could have come in no other way. For, although a great many cures have been wrought by people of slight understanding and little acquaintance with suffering, many cases have been reached only by these more sensitively organized people who have lived through the whole round of human ills, thereby learning how to cure or avoid them.

By some it is alleged that cures are wrought more rapidly by the Christian Science method of abstract faith, the denial of disease and the assertion of health, and that consequently it is better not to investigate, better not to admit any limitations. Yet the experience of the past fifteen years shows that such work is of temporary value only. Many through their enthusiasm perform remarkable cures for a time, then find themselves unable to heal, because they have no real understanding. Their teaching and work fly aloft like a rocket, and fall like a stick. Moreover, one has good reason to doubt if the "cures" really are cures; for actual facts are almost never procurable from a Christian Scientist. There was "nothing" troubling the patient in the first place: he was cured of "nothing," so there is nothing to relate. From such a point of view, there is naught to discuss. The truth in Christian Science will never be known until its fanaticism is eliminated; for it rests upon unsound foundations, and conceals a wealth of misstatement of which the public will some time be informed.*

Again, many have been helped by the silent method who have afterwards experienced a relapse. In some cases the relapse has been so great that the services of a regular physician have been required, while a few have been compelled to resort to medicine. The reason is evidently this: The mental cure may save life, and has done so in many hundred instances. It may give temporary relief, drive out pain, and cure superficial diseases. *But the only permanent remedy is understanding.* In the words of Dr. Quimby, "the truth, the explanation is the cure." This holds true of all methods of cure, of all methods of salvation, and of education: we progress permanently only so far as we understand.

Nearly every believer in the mental cure has passed through an abstract stage, where for a time mind was deemed capable of accomplishing everything. Prudence, common sense, and the laws of sanitation and hygiene were set aside; and there was a season of unlimited "revelry by night." But

---

* The practice of mental healing did not originate with the Christian Scientists, as has been claimed, but in the researches and practice of Dr. P. P. Quimby, of Belfast, Me. (1802-1866), who healed my parents, and also Mrs. Eddy, author of "Science and Health." See "The True History of Mental Science," by J. A. Dresser, The Metaphysical Publishing Company, New York, 1887; "The Philosophy of P. P. Quimby," by Annetta G. Dresser, Geo. H. Ellis, Boston, 1895. I have read all of Dr. Quimby's manuscripts, falsely reputed to be Mrs. Eddy's "first scribblings," in which the philosophy of mental healing is expounded for the first time. These manuscripts, written 1859-65, were the outcome of over twenty years' practice of mental healing.

invariably there has been a reaction, a return to common sense. The time must come when every Christian Scientist shall likewise be "brought low"; and, if some fall so far from the throne of abstract grace as to require the help of a regular physician, out of this severe lesson they will probably learn more wisdom than is contained in their entire philosophy of idealistic abstraction.

In fine, there is a lesson which common sense, individual thinking alone can teach. Each must understand his own temperament. Each must know how he caused his trouble, and learn by prudence and right thinking to avoid it. Self-help is the only permanent help; and, the sooner this begins, the better. The altruistic healer deems his educational work of far greater importance than the relief of suffering. He does not permit his patients to depend on him after they may be self-helpful. Nor does he continue to give treatment because of the money he may receive. He advises his patients to grasp the principle, and apply it for themselves. Hence those who reflect greatest credit on the cause are those who have received a few treatments, attended but few lectures, read a few books, and have then begun to learn the lessons of personal experience.

The radical and fanatical phase of the mental healing movement may therefore be deemed the forerunner of a genuinely rational system of spiritual therapeutics. The extreme doctrine was probably needed to stimulate thought, to awaken people from their servitude to material remedies. But, now that the awakening has come, the time is at hand for moderation and reason, for the union of forces wielded by mental healer and physician. For the two ought to work toward the same end. There is abundant need of the wisdom of both. On the one hand, the physician stands in need of the fresh investigations of the mental healer, while the healer is in sore need of greater physiological knowledge. Out of the researches of the two shall in due time grow a broader theory of disease and its cure. Out of their combined teaching shall come the wisdom which will show man how to prevent disease. And then the time will be close at hand when healthier children shall be born, when a higher consciousness and a purer body shall be the birthright of man.

When the strongest word in favor of mental treatment of another has been said, a sphere of work remains where patient evolution shall alone win the triumph. A time comes in the life of the individual when the healer's work is no longer effectual. The process of development has become more central, and the developing soul must take up the process for himself. This may involve a severe struggle at first,— for knowledge of the power of mind does not absolve one from responsibility in the contest for life,— it may mean the victory over a most intense nature or the long process of transmutation of the sex force; but, in the end, such an experience is the real solution of the problem of life. It is this individual struggle which translates theory into reality, which gives the soul true wisdom. Here the soul must walk alone for a season. Here it must display utmost patience, even be thankful that the experience has come, because of the high end that shall be achieved. The problem of spiritual healing thus becomes the problem of the spiritual life in general, and we have left the realm of disease for the domain of the soul's most trying opportunities. The supreme question then is: What is my place in life? "What wilt thou have me to do?" For the highest healing is love's supreme triumph. It is the dawning of the inner light, the beginning of the Christ-life, the complete dedication of the soul. Only he who enters this high realm shall know its full significance, only he shall accomplish the supreme work of the Spirit.

VI.

It is important, in connection with our study of spiritual healing, to consider the subtle mental influences known as thought atmospheres, at the same time considering methods whereby one can learn to control them. Every one knows more or less about these insidious influences, to be sure; yet, although we all suffer the consequences, we are often unconscious of the causes until our attention is called specifically to them. For, if people in general were acquainted with these influences, many diseases would be avoided, unhappy marriages would be far less frequent, to say nothing of the dishonest and immoral proceedings that would be stopped in the business and social worlds.

Every one knows that the atmospheres of cities, towns, and houses, vary according to the people who dwell there, and how hard it is to command one's self where the whole tendency is toward mere pleasure or money-getting or orthodoxy. Members of a household grow to think alike, not merely because they observe and imitate each other, but because they interchange thought atmospheres. Frequently two persons start to express the same thought simultaneously. Colds and other troubles run through a household. If one person feels depressed, others feel it, without knowing where their depression comes from; and a cheerful person will lighten an entire household by his mere presence. Clothing partakes of one's general condition, and it is sometimes easy to change the mind by making a change of clothes. Even the walls of a room seem to partake of one's mental state. At any rate, some are able to ease their minds by repapering and painting a house where a crime has been committed or where people have been ill. Atmospheres accompany letters, and the acute can read far more in this way than by written word. In fact, a letter seems to establish a connection between one mind and another, so that there is both give and take of invisible influence. If one enters a room in the dark, one can tell by the mental atmosphere whether or not a person is present there.

A similar instance of the association of thought with a material substance is that of food. One will eat and enjoy an unknown article of food until told its name,— something, perhaps, to which one has a natural repugnance; and after that one is unable to eat another morsel. Doctors know well that much more depends upon the patient's faith in medicine than in the medicine itself; and many times plain water or a simple white powder has wrought a cure, when the sufferer believed it to be a powerful drug.

The most startling discovery, however, is the extreme susceptibility of some minds to the subtle influences of more positive minds. Indeed, one sometimes asks if any soul really possesses itself, so close is our mental life to one another, so beset by hidden influences, suggestions, fears, and emotions. It is a most trying experience, from one point of view, to be conscious of these influences. Yet knowledge of them is the only protection for the sensitive mind, and the wisest course is to face the problem until it is solved.

I do not now refer to the "pressure" so often brought to bear externally,— such, for instance, as the immoral use of money, trickery, demagogism, alleged friendship, and the emotional effects practised by ministers. Every one has been swayed by emotion, and learned something concerning its persuasive power. Society has its eyes pretty well open to the phenomena of infatuation, and nowadays we have heard about hypnotism until we are tired of the word.

But thought influence has no such warning qualities as the stirrings of passion and emotion. It is deep, silent, and sly, and engages another mind to obey it in an entirely unsuspected way. Even those whose motives are good may use mistaken methods in the fulfilment of their aims. In such a case the mental effects are less likely to be known. Even "the elect" and the honest are deceived by this quiet persuasiveness; and, before one knows that there is a deep-laid scheme behind, the mind is brought into subjection to the suggestions of another. The influence may begin through mixture of mental atmospheres, or it may come simply by looking into the eyes of a dominating personality. Contiguity is responsible for many of these unsuspected effects. As I have already suggested, even mental treatment, if its laws are not understood, may be simply a mixing of atmospheres; and some have been made ill by permitting themselves to be "helped" by minds of a lower order. *One should never make one's self receptive to a person with whom one is not in spiritual affinity.*

Avoid approaching the thought transference stage with any one outside of the narrow circle of your well-tried friends. The unscrupulous sometimes make their desires known by this method. Young people think themselves in love, when the stronger mind is in reality dominating the weaker. Many a salesman disposes of goods to an unwilling customer because his thought is the stronger. Teachers who permit themselves to be idolized obtain a power over their followers for which their own weakness is responsible. Always one should guard the weakest side, and never reveal the secret of its weakness to a stranger. It is this weakest side which involves us in many of our difficulties, and we have reason to be grateful if we understand mental contamination in time to strengthen this side of our nature early in life.

Those who sit side by side in a lecture-room find after a time that they have been drawn together, and conversation follows as a matter of course. Every one has known people so deeply involved in an atmosphere that the persons were utterly unlike themselves, hypnotized, in fact, to think a witch a saint or a brute an angel. If people could know how wide the dominating influence of one personality can become, it would indeed be a most astounding revelation. There is nothing more fatal to healthy individual development than the acceptance of another's dogma as law. The mind is utterly closed to reason, and there is apparently no way to arouse such a mind to a sense of its servitude.

Concerning atmospheres in general, it seems probable that from each of us there is a sort of emanation, just as the odor emanates from a rose. Probably we are more or less affected by all people we meet with whom we have anything in common; that is, when we converse with them, write to them, or become *en rapport* with them. The orator creates an atmosphere by which his hearers are affected, according to their receptivity. The revivalist works upon his hearer's emotions, until through this forced and most lamentable process the ignorant are made to believe. In the same way one's sympathies are appealed to by suffering, when one is with the sick and sorrowful. Indeed, some find themselves so susceptible to mental influences that they are at times almost at the mercy of others' feelings. Frequently people are affected by two or three different atmospheres at a time, so that during a silent treatment the mind is freed from one person after another, until at last only the right individuality remains. In such cases the different atmospheres seem like layers, which are removed one after another.

One should, of course, exercise unusual caution to avoid such contamination as this. The safeguard is to set apart a little time each day to settle down to one's self, and the best way to throw off an unpleasant influence is of course to turn the attention toward one that is pleasant. Think, for instance, of some one whom you love, some one who is exceptionally pure or a person whom you greatly respect. Usually, it is sufficient simply to discover that one is involved in another's atmosphere, for the discovery leads to an act of will: one turns immediately from it. Even young people who are infatuated with each other would be freed if they could *know* that they are infatuated, if they could see themselves as they truly are.

To the acute mental healer little more is necessary in order to detect the real nature of a patient's trouble than to read the mental atmosphere, which, like any first impression, reveals that which may be otherwise concealed. In fact, the healer cares more to know what this atmosphere is, and whether it may be readily changed, than to know the nature of the disease. It is the disposition or temperament of the individual which has most to do with the patient's trouble.

What, then, is this atmosphere which emanates from a person, and which reveals so much that is otherwise hidden? Is it physical or mental? It seems to partake of both, for it reveals both the state of mind and of body; that is, besides the atmosphere surrounding people which we feel when near them, there is evidently a part of the mind which shades off gradually into brain and nerves. The thought put into the mind as a suggestion the night before, which has the power to awaken one at a given hour, evidently either becomes a physical state or at least gives rise to a physical state, calls the blood to the brain, and starts up the body into its waking condition. In the same way fear arouses a physical state and causes contraction of muscles and nerves. Anxiety takes off the flesh and wears deep lines in the face. Serenity makes the brow placid. Anger starts up heat, and often results in headache.

Is it not probable that, if the subconscious mind

could give forth all its knowledge, it would narrate in minute detail every slightest change that occurs in the body, every sensation we receive, every sound we hear, every thought we think, and every mental influence that comes to us? And would it not surprise us if we could learn of the impression left by every mind that brushed against us, so to speak? And what a wonderful process would be revealed, could we trace all the stages between a thought of fear or a word of love and its gradual retreat into subconsciousness, there to give rise to a physical change and register its effect in the nerve substance! As we elect to think, to suggest to ourselves, to believe, to become interested, so shall be the result in subconscious phenomena. That which we hold in consciousness at a given time is incomparably small when compared with the vast changes wrought below the threshold. Evidently, there is an unlimited possibility, enlarging outwards from this present moment. The only serious question is, Do we know where we stand, or are we deceived? If one is easily influenced, one must become acute enough to know when the influence takes place, and thus throw it off. But, most important of all, one must take care to live habitually in the right thought, that one may create a peaceful, health-giving atmosphere. Every experience will then be of benefit, if we meet it in the right spirit; and no atmosphere shall harm us if we keep free from fear. Our safety lies in understanding.

If, then, the question is asked, How can one free one's self from mental atmospheres and contaminations on the psychic plane? the answer is always the same; namely, understand whence and how they came. There was necessarily some point of contact, some channel left open. The point of contact may have been due to some weakened physical condition, in which case it is necessary to put the body in a pure, healthy state. One is concerned, not with the other person or persons, but with one's own state of mind and body, which made the mixing of mental atmospheres possible. Even if obsession be a fact, as some maintain, one has only one's own condition to blame, precisely as one should blame only one's self if, when another has used abusive language, one gets into a passion, and suffers all the torments of anger and hatred.

Hypnotism, too, is probably impossible unless there be (1) voluntary submission to hypnosis; (2) credulity which may be played upon; (3) a morbid, weakened, or diseased state of mind or body.* It is well, then, for all who are susceptible to external influences, to arouse the Cæsar in them, the conquering individuality which brooks no obstacle, and is capable of becoming master of the situation. Here is where the affirmative method

---

* See "The Psychology of Health and Happiness," La Forest Porter, M.D. Boston: The Philosophical Publishing Company. 1898.

is seen at its best. No weak attitude will suffice in such a case as this. One needs to stand up positively with all the power at one's command, and say emphatically: Never again, under any possible conditions, shall the sacred precincts of my personality be invaded by the atmospheres and feelings of other minds. I hereby declare my soul's independence. God and one make a majority; and I shall trustfully, yet positively, rest in the immanent presence, knowing that in that holy place I have nought to fear.

Vampires are numerous, and one must take care of one's self. One must respect and be strong in one's self in order to be respected, just as one must love to be loved. To take circumstances as they come, without discrimination, is positively immoral. One must be wise and exercise the power of choice, and champion the rights of the higher self. "You think me the child of my circumstances: I make my circumstance." Thus shall one grow strong in the face of all opportunities instead of weakening under them, if one takes this positive attitude, without nervous tension. It is of little avail to combat a mental influence. To rehearse the details of one of these subtle experiences is to become more deeply involved. A day spent alone with nature will often suffice to free one from the minds of others. Intellectual work is also helpful; and the more discriminative the thought, the more likely it is to restore a healthful tone to the mind.

If people try to control or subjugate me, I may rest calmly in my true self, in the love and peace, the power and protection, of the Father, and wait until their efforts cease. For nothing can touch the soul. All contamination is superficial. It does not affect the character. It is my own deed which moulds my character. If I send out hatred, if I retaliate, judge, condemn, or yield to the other's dominating spell, I consciously take part in the fray, and must suffer the consequences. If my feelings are hurt when a friend abuses me, it is because I descend to his level instead of sending out sentiments of charity and love. I have only to change my own attitude, be strong, self-reliant, and trustful of the higher power, to close the door to all influences.

I calmly think it over, thus realizing my powers of self-protection. I become grateful that this opportunity has come, that I have been attacked where I was weak, that this side of my nature has come to consciousness. If I take my opportunity now, this experience can never come to me again. If I calmly wait to let it settle itself without taking a hand in it, it will come to an end so much the quicker. Thus I quietly, but firmly, put myself in another attitude, in perfect forgiveness for the one who sought to influence me. Perhaps he is having an opportunity, too. The creative power is at work there, teaching him that the precincts of another mind are not to be invaded, that he cannot have things his own way. If I maintain this calm, forgiving attitude, it will help him to meet his problem. Is there any greater power in the world than this, the quiet, charitable, trustful attitude of soul where one sees the wisdom of the situation?

If one must live in a mental atmosphere of criticism and unjust demand, is it possible to maintain poise and health? This question suggests the complaint so frequently made that the circumstances in which we find ourselves placed are "too hard," and that, if we could live in a more favorable environment, all would be well. Yet, wherever we go, our problems follow us. The ideal conditions in which we would like to be placed would be thoroughly disappointing. It is here and now, in our present trying experience, that life's lesson may be best learned. And, whether the environment be harmonious or not, there is just as much need to maintain poise and individuality. Criticism may make the task harder for the time. But so much the better, if only one persists and faithfully concentrates upon an ideal, remembering that every experience means soul development. The persistent effort to realize the ideal will triumph in the end, despite all criticism, which in the end will be turned to good account, and, rightly received, will make one sweet-tempered.

But the question is still persistently asked, "How can I live according to the principles of spiritual healing among people who have no sympathy with the new principles?" It is easy for those who live continuously in the right atmosphere, it is said; but how are they to practise the new doctrine who have to meet the opposition of the world? The answer is the same as that to be made to any one who attempts to reform the world, to realize an ideal or live a better life; namely, be true to your best insight wherever you are. Quietly conform your life to it, refreshing yourself daily by the thought of the divine oneness, without talking much about it to people who are unsympathetic. Little by little people will observe the change, and will manifest far more interest in your new life than if you tried to convince them of the new truth. People will be impatient with you sometimes because you refuse to worry or to send for the doctor. But silent persistence on your part will make its impression some day. It is the life that tells, and there is no surer way to convince your friends that there really is something in your new ideas than by actual changes in conduct. It is better, on the whole, to permit those who delight in dosing to go on their way without trying to influence them directly. "If

Ephraim is joined to his idols, let him alone." People will not receive new ideas until they are ready; and, if one is too aggressive, one may arouse great antagonism.

Again, there is another strong reason for holding one's high belief and living up to it without attempting to teach except by example. If you are more open and developed interiorly than they, they will be quickened, helped, and strengthened, simply by your presence. There is no way in which one can help others more effectively than this, simply to be with them and to carry, not the sense of superiority, not the feeling that one has that which others lack, but the consciousness of the light and truth which is for all, regardless of personality.

While in one sense it is easier for those who live in a spiritually helpful atmosphere to practise these principles, on the other hand the greatest victories are won by those whose circumstances are most adverse. No one has learned the truth easily, but through very varied and often very hard experience. Apparently, no one can avoid experience; and, if one is spared trials with which others must contend, Nature invariably offers some fresh problem to solve. Those who consider the subject for the first time frequently say there is something which they cannot seem to grasp. They cannot at first apply the healing power. But this will always be so until one has tried. It is experience, even failure and renewed attempt, which conveys this elusive something.

One of the first evidences that one is effectively practising this method of development, by making full use of the subconscious mind and concentration upon the ideal or spirit, leaving outer effects to take care of themselves, is the gradual change in one's likes and dislikes. People whom one formerly cared for prove to be no longer congenial. One outgrows dogmas, beliefs, and books. In dress and desire for food, in one's amusements and social life, there is a gradual and instinctive change, betokening inner growth. In fact, there is no better way to elevate one's entire life than simply to develop spiritually, letting the outer change come about naturally and easily. For, if one tries to force one's growth and breaks off connections with people and things before one is ready, the change will not be permanent.

The problem of mental atmospheres is therefore the general problem of life in a new form. Probably a large part of the friction, and many of the diseases, as well as the majority of the subtle experiences we are now considering, could be avoided if man were to learn the great lesson of moderation, or the avoidance of extremes; if he would take as his motto, "Nothing to excess." In countless ways, and with a patient persistency which nothing could surpass, Nature does her utmost to warn us when we are approaching the normal limit, beyond which lie danger, misery, and insanity. Then she enforces her lesson by bringing upon us the reaction due to our own immoderate conduct. Yet we constantly disobey her mandates. Any one of these disobediences would teach us this secret of life's true economy.

The wise or economical method of adjustment to life is well illustrated by mountain-climbing. Observe a company of people making their first ascent, and you will see them start out with considerable energy, walking at a good rate of speed, and saying how easy it is to climb mountains. But very soon they find it necessary to slacken their speed, by and by they sit down for rest, drink considerable water, and then start out again, feeling stiff and somewhat discouraged about mountaineering. On the other hand, the Swiss guide who has climbed mountains all his life has sought out the easiest way. He assumes a steady pace, which he does not vary throughout the ascent. He drinks little or no water until the worst of the climbing is over. He does not sit down, but rests for a few moments at a time by quietly standing until he feels ready to resume the march.

The strong, erect attitude invites strength: the weakened, discouraged attitude increases the sense of fatigue. Here is an example which one might well follow throughout life. Life is, after all, very much like mountain-climbing, with its heights, its valleys, its sharp descents and glorious vistas. See the end, and then adjust yourself accordingly, resting not in a weak, but in a strong attitude, and you shall gather strength for the worst difficulties. When the pressure upon the muscles and nerves becomes too great, pause for a time until the organism is ready for more work. Pause in time, before the accumulation is too great to be easily thrown off. Disease comes from failure to observe this need of moderation, of rest and change of work; that is, it results from too much energy spent in one direction. It is temporary loss of poise. The pain is Nature's notification that she is trying to restore harmony; and, if one holds the right thought about it, one may rise above the sensation, quietly awaiting the time when one is ready to resume the habits of daily life. One may thus be a positive help to Nature, whereas a large part of our doctoring shows how utterly we neglect this beautiful law of life's economy.

There is one thought, therefore, of which we need constantly to remind ourselves, in the endeavor to apply the spiritual healing principle; namely, that every vital idea taken into the mind passes through a period of gestation. Particularly is this true when one receives new spiritual power. One seems to have retrograded and lost one's hold on the Power, when, as a matter of fact, it is working like leaven to leaven the whole lump. By and by one shall display habitually in daily life that which was at first a mere vision. But, when the vision fades and the clouds shut in again, its power has not gone. It is silently at work in subconsciousness to make us better, stronger, and healthier. Our conscious part is to await Nature's time, and not to think that we have degenerated.

VII.

One of the first conclusions reached by the general public, when told that the mind is the chief factor in the cause and cure of disease, is that disease is merely a "belief," or "idea." Consequently, people hope to please the disciples of the mental cure by saying that they have "the belief of a cold" or "the idea of a headache." Now, if disease were simply a belief, another belief might easily destroy it. In fact, some maintain that, as disease is wrong thinking, its cure is right thinking. In diseases of the imagination this may be true. But if, in general, beliefs were sufficient to cause disease, how soon we would think ourselves out of existence! We have fears enough in a day to put ourselves through all the ills of life, if by simply believing that we had them we should create them.

But it is evident that there is more in disease and its cure than this. When you take physical exercise, you do not merely believe that you are exercising. You have an idea which you carry into execution. You know that there is a vast difference between thinking and working. You are aware of the physical fact, of the movement of muscles and limbs. Likewise with pain. It comes involuntarily, not because you believe in pain. There is a difference between what you feel and what you think about your feeling. Suppose it is a burn. You can perceive the physical disturbance, feel the sensation coming from it; and you also have ideas in regard to it which may help or hinder its recovery. There are two sides, then, to physical pain. This is not our arrangement, but Nature's universal order. Everything we perceive in the outer world has two aspects,— that which is impressed upon us from without, despite our wills, and the state of mind it meets within.

Even in the case of hydrophobia, which is said on good authority to be a disease of the imagination, there is the shock to the mind caused by something external, the blanched cheek, and the other physical disturbances. In insanity, which is admitted by all to be a mental disease, there is invariably a disordered state of the brain, or too much power called in one direction; and in all mental maladies there is at least an accompanying disturbance of the nerves, if not of the vital functions. In the case of rheumatism, paralysis, dyspepsia, and the like, the physical disturbance is more marked than the mental.

It is clear that, in order to develop a consistent theory of disease, one must frankly admit all the facts, on the one hand, which the regular physician would describe as the symptoms and physical conditions of disease, and, on the other, the mental states and causes discovered by the mental healer. The physician deems the physical facts so important that, as a rule, he calls disease physical, and gives material remedies, regarding the state of mind as a sort of emotional accompaniment. The mental practitioner lays so much stress on the state of mind that the bodily disorder is looked upon as an effect. Thus the two stand squarely in opposition.

There should be full admission of all facts in regard to the physical side of life. It is here that the mental healer claims to have wrought such wonderful cures. It is because he finds the state of mind fundamental to the physical condition that he is able to reach cases where other methods of treatment have failed. Having admitted all the facts, he reserves the right to interpret them in his own way. Disease is defined as a state of the whole individual, beliefs, fears, sensations, and physical conditions being included in this general term.

It is an insufficient account of disease in plants and animals to affirm that it is due to close association with man. The mental healer has not yet offered an adequate explanation of purely physical disease. Nor is it at all rational to affirm that foods, drugs, and poisons possess such qualities only as man's belief gives them; for chemical substances obviously possess qualities of their own, qualities whose ultimate basis is to be found, not in man's intelligence, but in the creative mind of God. It is equally vain to assert that denizens of the northern hemisphere are stricken with fever when they visit the tropics, because of mere belief in or fear of it. The cause lies deeper than this; and, if the mental healer seeks a purely mental explanation of the troubles incident to climatic changes, this question, together with the diseases of plants and animals and the qualities of matter, must long remain an unsolved problem.

Owing to the wide-spread prevalence of this theory that disease is a "belief," it is customary among advocates of the New Thought to ask, "What have you been thinking?" when told that one is suffering from some disease. But here again the trouble is as likely to be of physical as of mental origin. There may be an accumulation of heat, fatigue, or impurity which Nature is seeking to throw off, in which case the disturbance is obviously physical. Thought may greatly hinder or help the process. Out of a slight trouble of this sort, fear, doctoring, and the like can create "real" disease. Or, if one understand Nature's recuperative process, the right thought may co-operate with and greatly assist Nature. But the mind is in such a case clearly the directive, not the originating power. Everything depends upon the kind of thought held at the outset. The actual disturbance, however, is physical.

The critic may reply that the cause was mental. It was, of course, the mind's fault that one went to excess, thus bringing on Nature's remedial reaction. But the accumulation, the actual trouble, is physical. The immediate occasion was a physical habit, a wrong way of living. Disease is the result of our way of living, mentally and physically. Its cure must come by understanding our defects of conduct, physical as well as mental, and by the gradual remedying of them through the application of greater wisdom : it can come in no other way. The simple reason why many who have received mental treatment have relapsed into their former condition, or experienced only a slightly permanent benefit, is because thought alone is insufficient. It is not enough to become a convert to the New Thought. The life must be altered. This means not only a change of thought, but of habit; and habit is largely physiological. This is simply common sense, and one has but to consider it to accept it unqualifiedly.

Do not, therefore, if you would really know the truth, hold to an abstract theory, refusing to consider the possibility of a physical aspect of disease. Value facts above theory. Ask first, What are the actual conditions, regardless of any theory I wish to prove or disprove? Then, having ascertained the facts, ask how the conditions can best be remedied by a change of thought and physical life. Seek the cause in physico-psychical life. Learn how by giving the forces of the body the wrong direction you enter into and intensify sensation, how by turning in the opposite direction you help Nature. There is no permanent remedy except that which comes through the individual. Just as truly as "only thyself thyself canst harm," so only thyself thyself canst cure. Freedom from disease shall come at last through understanding of its total origin, and a part of that is always in one's inmost self.

Again, many disciples of the new doctrine object most strenuously to the use of physical remedies. But, while knowledge of the power of thought is in its infancy, why not employ the best means at hand? If a person is suffering acutely, there must be immediate relief; and common sense dictates that we use those aids to physical recovery which men have found most useful in the past. And what wonders Nature can accomplish during sleep, what efficacy in the use of hot and cold water, in the right kind and amount of food!

Some have also objected to the gymnasium, on the ground that one must accomplish everything through mind. But how else could one exercise the body except through mind? Is not consciousness always fundamental? Does not a physical change always accompany the thought process? How, then, is one neglecting the mind by exercising it through systematic gymnastic development? Is not he who puts the right thought into his physical exercise the one who is likely to gain the fullest benefit from his work?

It is a fact, which every one may as well frankly admit, that the mind expresses itself fully and harmoniously only when the body is in good condition. Instances are on record where, in cases of suspended animation, the mind has been powerless to move a muscle, although the persons were conscious of everything that was going on about them. People are frequently blamed for surliness and impatience in disposition, when they are suffering from some persistent physical inharmony which, when removed, would take away an obstacle to the power of mind and improve the disposition. In fact, if we could simply remove all obstacles of this sort, it is probable that this objective method alone would suffice to heal the mind of a large part of its inharmonies. But let one adopt the principle that all these methods are good in their special fields, and one may by right use of ideal suggestion,* by the experience in the silence, by wise physical exercise, and by judicious development of all sides of one's nature, become rounded out,

---

* By far the ablest treatment of this subject is Henry Wood's "Ideal Suggestion Through Mental Photography," Boston, Lee & Shepard.

healthy, and strong to a degree impossible of attainment to the extremist. Common sense is a safe guide, wherever we go; and he who would rather die for a principle than try another's method cares more for abstract theory than for universal truth.

Is it not, then, entirely a question of the idea which regulates action? If I were to help myself by working upon sensation alone, I should become morbid and discouraged. But, if I carry with my direction of mind the thought of the divinity within every particle of my being, I may place my consciousness anywhere, and uplift the lowest that is in me and make it pure. An affirmation or suggestion may help at the outset, and the affirmation may be true as an ideal. Yet this method is but a stepping-stone to realization, the habitual recognition of the divine ideal immanent in the real. Let me start each time with this thought, and all my conduct shall be gradually lifted to the plane of the Highest.

That the effect produced upon us by pain and pleasure in general depends upon the attitude with which we meet them is clear from the commonest experiences of life. Suppose, for example, I am suffering from long-continued pain, and have worked myself into a most distracted state of mind through fear. Suppose, too, in order to make out the best case for the tyrant fear, I communicate my misgivings to friends and strangers as in general my belief about myself. Let me now sit down quietly, and honestly ask myself: Now what do I really believe? Do I sincerely think all these calamities are coming upon me? Or am I pretending to fear that which my true self denies? After careful consideration, to my joy, I find that I really believe all my fears are absurd. In fact, I have a firm conviction that I shall escape these supposed terrors. I actually laugh at my fears. What a magical effect this change of mind has! With what a different spirit I approach life!

The conclusion of such thinking is that belief alone is not sufficient to kill or cure. It is discord of action that brings disease. Pain is an evidence that we have spent our energies to excess in some direction, that we must slacken our pace and rest. Instead of affirming that we are in good condition, common sense tells us to take means to place ourselves there. If you are nervously inclined, do not then affirm that you are poised, but act, take hold of yourself, remove the tension, and live more moderately. The cultivation of thought is for the purpose of teaching man how to act; for action, not thought, is of primary importance. Since disease has come by acting contrary to Nature's laws, its cure must come by obedience to them, by wise conduct. Thought and deed must therefore go hand in hand, and out of their union shall come the healthier life.

Many a case is on record of invalids suddenly cured when they were unexpectedly spurred to action; for example, the rescue of some one in danger or the escape from a burning building. A physician once entered an invalid's room flourishing a carving-knife, and, in order to start her into the activity which resulted in her cure, declared that he would cut his patient's throat unless she rose from her bed.* The essential is some experience which shall make a vivid impression, leading the sufferer to make that move which no one can make for her. For the energy is quiescent, potential, and must be made kinetic, just as one might rouse from one's restful position by the window and hasten to save the life of some one in danger in the street.

The difficulty is like a problem in physical science. There is a certain weight to be moved. The question is how to apply energy. It may be compared to an attempt to move a heavy cart. The strong man applies his shoulder to it, but it does not move. He tries again and again, until finally a slight movement results. When the cart is once started, it is easier to maintain its motion. Likewise in self-help the difficulty is to begin, to rouse from apathy, from absorption in sensation and self-consciousness, to push out from within,

---

* For similar instances of sudden cure, see "Facts and Fictions of Mental Healing," by C. M. Barrows, Boston: H. H. Carter; "Influence of Mind upon the Body," by Daniel Hack Tuke, M.D.,—a very able treatment of the subject.

just as one might cheer up if a dear friend whom one had not seen for many months should come suddenly into the room. That which has many times happened accidentally, one can learn to repeat by self-conscious methods, creating from within the activity needed to start the system into renewed life.

If, therefore, you find yourself settling into despondency, fear, worriment, sensation, self, with a lurking suspicion that the worst is yet to come, say to yourself: "Attention! This has gone far enough. I will endure it no longer. I have tolerated fears in which I have no real credence, and adjusted myself to aches which must have no place in my life. I have felt ill because I have thought too much of myself, nursing sensation as if it were a joy. This day shall witness a change in my thought and in my life. This day shall prove that I am master, and not slave."

Thereupon one should begin to make active effort, for mere affirmation will not suffice. Take positive hold of yourself, of the higher Power. Then apply such power as your thought can direct, in an active, quickening manner. Open from within, open upward in thought, until the brain responds, as you would throw open the blinds and look out of a house. Start an enlivening, awakening thrill through the entire physical system, and help the body to respond by animated movements, as though you really were *alive*, not merely feigning life.

Or, if the case be not so serious, apply the activity in a more quiet way, by starting a series of expanding impulses from the solar plexus, the nerve centre which most quickly responds to therapeutic thought. Sometimes these solar plexus impulses come in rhythms, or beats of three, followed by a long breath, and possibly a sneeze, showing that the circulation of the blood has become more active. The thought of peace! peace! as of a quiet power applied to a disturbed nervous centre to free it from tension, is sufficient to carry the blood down from the head until the feet are warmed. Thus one is conscious of a bodily response, while the direct thought is withdrawn from the body, and focused upon the inner activity, the awakening and hopeful thought which causes the new response.

It is of great practical advantage, therefore, to regard disease in the light of disturbed action rather than as erroneous thought, and, accordingly, to apply the active spiritual power, guided by thoughts of hope, *energy*, *life*. One may well afford to let beliefs and fears pass in and out of mind, like harmless spectres, while concentrating one's attention on the central problem of life; namely, the meaning and nature, the possibilities and use, of the power of individual action. It is the thought accompanied by the deed that is effective, not the mere idea. No theory of mental healing is adequate which does not thus take account of that which is even more fundamental than thought. In the analysis and development of the power of activity is, in fact, to be found the inmost clew to the meaning and perfecting of life.*

*See "Man's Place in the Cosmos," by Professor Andrew Seth. Edinburgh: Blackwood. 1897. For a fuller statement of the philosophical system implied in the doctrines of spiritual healing, see "The Spirit of Modern Philosophy," Professor Royce, Houghton, Mifflin & Co. 1892. The theory that the soul has a spiritual existence aside from its passing states of consciousness has been very elaborately considered in Lotze's great work, "Microcosmus," translated by Elizabeth Hamilton and E. E. C. Jones. Edinburgh: T. & T. Clark. 1885.

VIII.

ANOTHER respect in which the current theory of spiritual healing is susceptible of progress is in the wider acceptance and application of the philosophy of evolution. Although its leading exponents already believe the theory of evolution to be the only plausible hypothesis of the creation of things, a large percentage are still disbelievers in it, while it is not uncommon to hear or to read an attempted refutation of it.* This is due partly to misapprehension of the meaning of evolution, and partly to lingering belief in the old dogmas of creationism. In order to point out the benefit that would follow from a broader application of the evolutionary philosophy, let us first consider what sort of evolution the believer in ultimate spiritual reality is likely to accept.

Evolution as described by men of science is in large part a record of physical changes, the events which have characterized the past history of the earth and the appearance of the various organisms and species which have led to man. It is an en-

* Evolution is sometimes rejected because of its supposed necessary connection with the doctrine of reincarnation, an entirely different theory. Such an attempt is "God Incarnation *versus* Personal Reincarnation, Evolution and Karma," by M. E. Cramer. San Francisco: Harmony Publishing Company. 1898.

deavor to read the history of creation on the outside.

Thus considered, the science is still far from complete; and the most important problems yet remain unsolved. On the other hand, evolution as considered by philosophy is an interpretation of life's history in terms of ultimate Being, or the immanent Power, the resident Energy, whose omnipresent life or activity is the immediate cause of the changes which evolutionary science describes. Science observes the details, and is little concerned with their ultimate background. Philosophy considers the fundamental Power, and awaits the catalogue of details, as rapidly as they shall be gathered by science. Science must know the widest possible data exemplifying the law. Philosophy sees in the law the explanation of the details.

In the light of this endeavor to comprehend evolution at large and in detail, we may define the principle, as the law whereby the forms, complexities, and beings of to-day have progressively come into existence, the law by which the progressing beings, minds, and societies of to-day are becoming the more highly developed products of to-morrow. Evolution means transformation, recreation, growth. Its activity does not call for creation of force, it does not mean its annihilation. It is simply the living tendency, the mutation of that which eternally exists. It is a march from lower to higher, from lowest to highest, from simple to complex, by a gradual process of modification, not by interference from without, but by stimulation or quickening from within. There is no need of an external creator, only the existence of a resident, progressing Power, moving within us, and carrying onward to remoter ends that which already exists. Every change on the surface of things is, therefore, evidence of this progressive activity. Every slightest modification is a revelation of God, the only God in whom the student of evolution can believe. Its outlook is toward the future,— a future whose nature may, for all we know, be in part undetermined. It regards the past as the parent of the present, not as a time when God was any more active than now. Its ideals are gradually formulated ideals, slowly realized. It is perpetual flux, except so far as law and the sum total of force are concerned. Its power is universal, owning matter and consciousness, things and ideas alike. It is the great becoming, achieving life of the universe, the progressive revelation of God.

Thus broadly considered, there is not an atom, not a star, not an accident, nor a purpose, that lies outside of its sphere. It is the greatest revelation the human mind has ever made ; and, from the time of the general discovery and proclamation of the law, every branch of knowledge has gradually been falling into line, all thought has been revolutionized, and naught can stem its resistless tide. It is opposed by those only who as yet fail to comprehend it. It is incontestably the only hypothesis which in any way accounts for the development of life; and, while its application must be the work of many generations, the acceptance of the law as the true explanation is among thinking minds no longer matter of dispute.* If our knowledge of it has not yet explained all the mysteries, the discovery of the law has at least put us on the right track. It has taught us not to dogmatize, but to evolve with evolution, and learn what the universe shall become when the grand ideal is actually achieved. It finds a place for all our cherished, at least for all our sanest, ideals. It is not hostile to the spiritual life. It does not contradict our faith in free, achieving man. It is the universe of opportunity, it is the realm and basis of hope.

Let us now consider how this great law, the theory of a free, progressive man, living in an evolving universe, carried forward by an immanent God, applies to the realization of the ideals of spiritual healing.

In the first place, if permanency is only relative,

---

*For a fuller statement of the doctrine of evolution see "Evolution and its Relation to Religious Thought," by Professor Joseph Le Conte, D. Appleton & Co.; "The Destiny of Man," by John Fiske, Houghton, Mifflin & Co.; "Our Heredity From God," by E. P. Powell, D. Appleton & Co.

we have no assured knowledge of ultimate ideals. There may be an archetypal man, the perfect ideal or Christ. But few men as yet agree in regard to it. It is futile to quote the Christian Bible as authority, since people are unable to agree in their interpretations of it. In truth, each man's ideal is no greater than his own wisdom enables him to conceive. The ideal moves forward with the development of those who conceive it. The utmost one can accomplish in the endeavor to help another is to hold up the perfect type, as one chances to regard it at the time. By restating the ideal each time, ever seeking to picture it more clearly and beautifully, by regarding the omnipresent Spirit as even now engaged in realizing a progressive ideal, one may keep pace with evolution, and hold an ideal that is ever fresh and strong.

How long a time has elapsed since the truth of evolution became known! yet we still have with us the old dogma that man was created perfect, and fell. We still look toward the past, trying to read there the lineaments of perfection, to recover the beauties of the golden age. The philosophy of spiritual healing has been greatly burdened by this dogma. The entire practice of mental cure is hampered by it. It is the mill-stone of theology, the enemy of progress, the dirge of despair.

Evolution knows nothing of a past golden age. It points to the past only as the chrysalis out of which the progressing present has come. All that it logically permits us to say is that the present may, by our united efforts, give rise to a better future, which may in turn lead to somewhat better than that. The ideals of to-day will become the food and drink of conservatives to-morrow. The morality and spirituality of this age will be transcended by that of the next, and thus onward, *ad infinitum*. The only rational ideal, therefore, is experimental, tentative, progressive: the only rational method of attainment is the endeavor to take the next step in evolution.

That this is not the usual method of mental healers is evident from the continued use of suggestions like the following: "I am eternally perfect," "I am master of the body and all its functions."

In support of these assertions, it is affirmed that to make the suggestion, even though it be untrue, is to help it become a fact. There is a truth here, as we have recognized in the foregoing pages. But the experience of the past decade, during which this method of statement has been so much in vogue, shows that, while thousands have been helped by these ideals, many have worked themselves into a high-strung nervous condition, from which it was necessary to seek relief by other means. It would seem wise, therefore, to modify the suggestions, so that they shall not involve untrue assumption, but aid the thought in moderate co-operation with evolution.

Let us examine one of these assertions, in order to discover what it means. "I rule the body and all its functions." In the first place, we do not consciously rule the body; for its functions are largely reflex or unconscious. It is better thus; and, if one tries to control a function,— for example, the operation of the heart,— one may suspend the activity too long, as did the man who learned to control his heart, but one time exceeded the lawful limit, and stopped its beating forever. The functions of the body demand adjustment on our part rather than interference. He who, like a certain hypnotist of whom I know, suggests that the number of pulse-beats be diminished or increased, or who tampers with the natural rhythm of any of the organs, may maim a person for life.

Secondly, if one were really master of the body, the brain would be under perfect control. But who controls, save in a slight degree? How shall this control ever be attained, except through gradual intellectual development? The sex force would also be under entire subjection or be entirely transmuted. What a millennium! What a victory!

I need not multiply examples to show that in some respects adjustment is wise,— in some cases, control,— and that the rational method of attaining control is not the assumption that we possess it now, but the question, How far have I advanced in evolution? What degree of self-control have I already attained? For the understanding of wherein and why I fail will best show me how to take the forward step. It is of no avail to affirm that I do succeed, that there are no failures. Humility and understanding, not assumption and self-satisfaction, lead to progress.

But, it is maintained, there is a point of view from which the affirmation of perfection is true, in reality the soul is always free or whole, all is perfect, all is good, while seeming evil or imperfection is an illusion. Then why should there be evolution? Is not this theory of the abstract absolute an utterly unwarrantable assumption? In the light of evolution the soul is now in process of attaining wholeness, we are on the road to perfection, all shall become good when all become moral and spiritual. As a matter of fact, when we descend from the heights of theoretical abstraction, we must admit that we know life only from the present, relative point of view, where man feels, thinks, and suffers according to his state of development. Even though I ascend to the "superconscious" plane, my experience is still mine, relative and imperfect. I have beheld visions of ideal conditions; but that does not alter the fact of my present undeveloped condition, a state which I can remedy only by understanding it, through gradual evolution.

I must therefore decide which form of statement is true. Shall I, in the valley, affirm that I am on the mountain top, or shall I recognize where I am, and aspire to stand upon the summit? I cannot be in both places at once. The statements that two and two make four, and two and three make four, are not both true. I may believe that I shall eventually stand upon the mountain summit, — that is rational, — but I can do so only by taking each step leading to it. If I am imperfect, I am not perfect; and it is untrue to assume perfection. For, if I am perfect, evolution is an illusion; and I need not try to take the next step. If, however, evolution is a fact, it is real, it bears some relation to ultimate Being, miscalled the Absolute.

An absolute point of view would be a fixed standpoint, all would be eternally perfect, there would be no change, no novelty, no progress, no sphere of development, no moral order, no freedom, no ethical selves, no finite life at all. If this be so, the finite will is "fictitious," we are "forced" by suffering to grow, there is no meaning or purpose in life. This is, in fact, what many believers in this abstract theory hold to be true. The abstract is the real, the concrete is illusory and unmeaning. There is no purpose in our suffering; the Absolute does not know it at all.

To argue that because people have always believed in the Absolute, therefore this abstraction is a reality, is no valid reason for belief in it. People universally believed the earth to be the centre of the universe, until Copernicus showed them their error. An enthroned, king-like God was once believed to exist, until the philosophy of evolution compelled him to abdicate. And now another Copernicus, in the shape of many philosophers, points out the truth that all we know about God is the power which evolution reveals, that the Absolute is a myth, and God, or reality, is what our progressive experience proves him to be.*

Shall one, then, settle into the consciousness of imperfection? Shall the thief call himself a thief? That would be untrue to moral evolution, which says, Recognize your misdeed for what it is, do not excuse it, but bring before your mind the consciousness of a better self than the present one. Hold to the practical ideal. Aspire with evolution, formulate the type to which evolution seems to be tending, and learn by a study of the conditions how to take the next step. The perfect is yet to be. No one has yet beheld its sublime lineaments. A part of me aspires to be perfect. I will therefore think of that. I am not wholly a thief. I have also a self in me that tells me it is wrong to steal. That self I ought to obey.

* See "The Will to Believe," by Professor James. Longmans, Green & Co. 1897.

I am not wholly sick. Accordingly, I will focus my thought elsewhere than on the part that is sick. I will take all wise means to become wholly well. But I will avoid all nervous tension that would arise from the affirmation that I am already at the goal. Is not the fact that many who have received mental treatment, and afterwards have relapsed to their former condition, due to their temporary assumption of health, when, in truth, they had not yet attained the goal? Must not all who now dwell on the abstract heights some time come to judgment, frankly admit where they stand, how egoistic assumption has hindered their growth? Is there any permanent or healthy growth, except that which comes gradually, as we patiently understand each detail, consciously take each step?

In a recent mental healing magazine I read: "To every suggestion of evil in your daily life, mentally declare, There is no evil. To all talk about evil, such as scandal, descriptions of disease, accounts of death, disaster, fears, discouragements, and danger, silently say, That is not true. Many cases have been healed by that simple, silent message."

But of what avail to say of the facts of social vice or of the Armenian atrocities, for instance, that "they are not true," "there is no evil"? Alas! the world knows too well that they are true, that there is evil; and it is useless to make denials. The problem of life will never be solved until we know why such things can be. The world will not be wholly beautiful until their cause has been destroyed. It will require somewhat beside negations to uproot it. It must be persistently recognized as an outrageous blot upon the universe, and not smoothed over by "beautiful metaphysics," not ignored by the glib philosophy that "all is good."

Again I read elsewhere that, "since in God there is no evil, I deny that there is any reality to evil at all. There is no real power in sin or death." Yet, since there is actual evil in the world, evil is known in the consciousness of God. The God who knows nothing of evil is as purely a myth as the Creator who made man perfect, then allowed him to fall. The only logical God is he whose consciousness embraces just this struggling, evolving, imperfect world which you and I would like to see freed from evil. There is real power in sin and death; and this energy we hope to turn, God helping, into a better channel. For it is the resident force of all evolution.

Once more I read: "I am free! I am free from doubt, I am free from care. I am the free and fearless, impersonal, selfless child of God; and what I am, so are you, my neighbor, as myself." The whole contention of my argument is that we are not yet free, and may become so only by awakening to consciousness of our servitude. I do not wish to be impersonal or selfless, but become more and more my individual self. And, as for being free from doubt, the coming of vigorous doubt would be the best event that could befall the philosophy of spiritual healing. Had doubt come hand in hand with belief, these moss-grown dogmas would long ago have been cast aside.

What is needed, therefore, in order to free the new faith from creationism and its attendant beliefs, is downright criticism. It is to the absence of healthy criticism that a large part of its irrationalities are due. Yet the majority of its followers are so convinced that all criticism is fault-finding or hatred that they turn away in dogmatic self-complacency even from the comments of those who have its welfare most at heart. True criticism, however, is both negative and positive: it reveals both defects and possibilities. It is inspired by love. It doubts only because it has caught glimpses of a higher ideal. It is sceptical in statement when, by so speaking, it may stimulate thought.

In this spirit, one would like to see the postulates of the mental healing philosophy subjected to the severest scrutiny. Instead of continually affirming that man was "created perfect," "There is no evil," "I rule the body," "I am free," one should now and then ask: Is there a valid reason for making these statements? What do they imply? Am I affirming mere theory, or speaking from actual knowledge?

The result would be the development of a method accomplishing a much greater amount of good, because its statements would be true and appeal to reason. Instead of affirming that "I rule the body," "I am free," "There is no evil," the disciple of the New Thought would then say: "I will keep before me the ideal of freedom until, in the course of evolution and the discovery of the cause of misrule, the body shall be in every normal respect my servant. I long to be free. I believe freedom to be my right. I will therefore hope, aspire, believe, at the same time trying to discover where, through ignorance, I still deprive myself of freedom. I believe, too, in the goodness of things. I will that the good shall triumph. There shall be no evil. I will do my part toward its elimination by first becoming better myself, more unselfish, more loving, by becoming truly free, truly self-masterful, truly wise."

In order to make this point perfectly clear, let us consider yet further the rational substitute for this abstract system of statement. I discover in myself some blemish of character or imperfection of body. According to the abstract method I ought to say to myself: "I am made in the image of God. God is perfect. Therefore, this imperfection is a shadow. I deny its existence. My character is unspotted. My body is the temple of the living God."

But, according to the philosophy of progress, I find an upwelling Life within me, which, I believe, is working for my good, for my perfection. I will therefore try to become more conscious of its moving, that I may learn whither it is tending. I will use my brain, that I may understand and control it. I will harmonize my thought with the natural rhythm of my bodily functions. I will try to be true (although I may frequently fail) to the highest wisdom of the moment, thereby developing character. I will exercise my body, and make it consciously the temple of the living God. I hope some time to master myself; but, understanding that all valuable possessions come gradually, I do not expect suddenly to become perfect. I expect to learn as much from failure as from success. I do not ask to become precisely like my present ideal, only to move toward that ideal, hoping that, long before I realize it, a far nobler ideal shall take its place. My present imperfection is not a shadow: it is an undeveloped portion of my real self. It is an aspiration, a hope. Therefore, I will take courage.

I seem to be of worth to the universe. In the universe I find law, order, progress. As I hope, as I aspire, as I labor, so shall the result be. I will not, therefore, waste time by claiming to be what I am not, but throw myself in line with evolution, begin where I am to-day and prepare for the morrow. I will be patient and wait, trying to understand myself better each day. So thinking and so doing, I am confident that nothing shall defeat me. I will earn the right to freedom by thinking myself out of slavery. There is every reason in the world why I shall succeed; for man is a responsible, active agent, life has a meaning, fate is what I choose, and God himself cannot refuse the gifts which he has taught us through nature how to obtain.

It is important, therefore, again and again to ask the definite question: Which point of view is the true one, that of the theoretical Absolute or of the actual finite? Shall one posit the existence of a perfect, immutable God, unaware of evil, then proceed to the universe, and find it perfect now? Arguing in this way, a Hindu sage says, "The creation of the universe is only explicable as due to the power of illusion: otherwise, the immutability of Brahma would be questioned; for the *non esse* can never give birth to anything real." Or shall we start with life as we find it, and proceed to the logical, immanent God? The issue is sharp and unmistakable. Everything depends upon the premises we adopt. If the abstract point of view be the true one, the argument in regard to evil is right: There is no evil: the soul is perfect. I rule my body. All is good. We are all happy and satisfied. There is no progress, nothing to do and nothing to hope for. If it is wrong, these logical conclusions are wrong, the assertive method is wrong. There is actual evil, there is progress, we are not yet satisfied, there is everything to do, everything to hope for.

In each case, therefore, where we seem to lose by surrendering the old faith, we are offered the alternative of the philosophy of evolution. Before some one thus tested creationism, it was easy to believe that God created the world out of nothing, and pronounced it "good." Then some one asked, How could this be? and it proved unthinkable. In the same way, every abstraction proves unthinkable when we apply it to the problems of actual life; for actual life, not theoretical perfection, is the true reality.

The methods and beliefs of the mental cure, when thus put to the test, evolve into the broader affirmations of a consistently progressive philosophy. For the principle is true. It is the affirmation, the ideal or prayer, which shapes our evolution, and heals. The practitioner of the New Thought is using the evolutionary power when he helps himself or another. But his words are often as inconsistent as are the orthodox hymns sung by Unitarian congregations. Whereas, if the whole of life is in forward movement, entire human life and thought should be in harmony with it. Man is a progressive being, and should be approached, helped, regarded as such.

Look upon all men, therefore, as centres of progress. Do not think so much of what they have been, of what they are, as of what they may become. Regard even their faults as aspirations for the perfect, and help them to evolve. Do not arrive at fixed, pessimistic conclusions concerning them. It is very discouraging to suffer from the thought of those who have thus made up their minds about us. But hope for the best. It is not too much to expect that every wrong shall be righted, that even the worst family feuds shall be adjusted. Therefore believe yourself, believe all people, to be on the road to freedom, health, happiness, and peace. Hold those thoughts about them and about yourself which are most practical,— not the abstract, assumptive ideal, but the thought which concerns itself with the nearest step in progress. Help people to express themselves, help them to think progressive thoughts. Try to free thought and conversation from all vestiges of the dogmas of creationism. Think out and apply the philosophy of evolution until your entire mental life shall be consistent with it. Turn the face toward the future, and build in creative imagination the golden age, the paradise, the heaven yet to be.

Thus shall our theory of healing become truly spiritual; for it shall harmonize with the idea of the immanent, achieving Spirit. It shall throw aside the garments of orthodoxy, creationism, fatalism, and all that now encumbers it, and become broadly progressive. Its highest endeavor shall be to realize the inspiration of the moment. "Not my will but Thine, be done,"— not my ideal but the ideal of the Father, who reveals himself as rapidly as man is ready.

The future of the philosophy of spiritual healing, therefore, depends upon its choice of either the abstract or the evolutionary method of thought. As long as so many of its advocates assume that it is already an exact science and art, while they continue to build upon the airy foundation of the Absolute, to assert "the I," and to assume perfection and omniscience, the movement will not grow. If it shall continue to sympathize with Orientalism, to inculcate fatalism, and ignore ethical distinctions by affirming that "all is good," its life will be anything but progressive. But, when it begins to admit its failures, to confess its ignorance, to learn of the philosophy of evolution, the moral idealist, and the physician, and to eliminate absolutism, then it will take a new lease of life, will appeal to men of science, and enter a greatly enlarged sphere of helpfulness.

But, in the endeavor to reduce the phenomena and practice of mental healing to a science, let us not neglect the spiritual life, the real outcome of these abstract thought methods which we have been criticising. The true object of spiritual healing is the liberation of the soul. All other ideals are secondary to this. All methods are of minor consequence as compared with the experience which touches this inmost heart of life. He who is conscious of the soul's union with the Father may calmly and trustfully take his stand upon this foundation, and let all else respond. He who is thus grounded heals by his presence, and has no need of any particular method of cure.

In life as a whole, then, there is a gradual transition from external methods to the inmost attitude of spiritual self-command. First the body is cared for by physical means, then through the power of thought. For a time one is helped by silent treatment, then the time comes when self-help alone avails. The process changes from physical to mental, from mental to spiritual. The object at first is relief from physical suffering. In the second stage the desire to grow is the governing ideal. Finally, one is not so eager to be free from suffering as to learn its full lesson, not so eager to grow as to realize the eternal realities of life in whatsoever condition one is placed.

But, if one could tell what it means to live wholly

in the spirit, and let all healing come as it will, one could continuously abide there. What soul in the flesh has attained this high level, where there is utter superiority to, complete independence of, all physical sensation? One who should have attained this poise would scarcely need to remain longer in the flesh. We are all striving for it. We are all endeavoring to throw off the bondage of sense. Yet how great the undertaking, which demands not only complete control of physical sensation, but entire mastery of self! One can sometimes attain this poise for a few moments. Then how deep and swift the result! All other moments seem trivial in comparison. Yet the right to such power and peace must be earned through patient plodding and experiment, through failure and struggle. All that leads the way to it is obviously necessary. The response would be too rapid if one could always attain this marvellous self-command. Therefore, have patience, our wiser self seems to say. The spirit is most responsive, the mind is far more moderate, and the body infinitely slow as compared with the movement of the spirit. While we are in the body, we must accordingly adjust ourselves to the laws of physical nature. It is unwise to apply pressure to the body beyond certain very moderate limits. The body's methods of response are far healthier than any you may impose upon it.

Learn of your body, therefore, and move forward with its rhythm. Half our ills are due to impatience. There is an infinite source of help in simple repose, in the restfulness of the nerves. While one is thus reposing, from far depths within the spirit shall speak, the Father, the infinite Love, the Christ. To hear this calmest whispering, this it is to be healed. To turn from sensation and self to that which owns and transcends all, this is the supreme endeavor, this suggests the exalted experience our words would express, if possible, this is the soul's true freedom, this the greatest joy of life.

APPENDIX A.

TOPICAL OUTLINE FOR FURTHER STUDY.

A. *The Nature of Matter.*

1. Atomic theory. Materialism. Lange's "History of Materialism."
2. Theory of psychic atoms. Van Norden, "The Psychic Factor."
3. Philosophical Idealism. Berkeley. Kant. Royce, "The Spirit of Modern Philosophy."
4. Primary and secondary qualities, their relationship and origin.

B. *The Relationship of Mind and Matter.*

1. Physiological psychology. Titchener, "An Outline of Psychology." (See a refutation by Professor A. Seth, "Man's Place in the Cosmos," Chap. III.)
2. Parallelistic hypothesis, no interaction.
3. Theory of intermediary action.
4. Subconscious mind and unconscious cerebration.
5. Rajah Yoga philosophy compared with the discoveries of mental healing. Swami Vivekananda.

C. *Thought Transference.*

1. Wave-motion theory.
2. Theory of psychic transfer from disembodied spirits. (See the Proceedings of the Society for Psychical Research.)

D. *Subjective Mind Theory.*

1. Hudson's "Law of Psychic Phenomena," its limitations and value. See also his "Scientific Demonstration of a Future Life."
2. Solipsism. (See Bradley, "Appearance and Reality.")

E. *Theories of the Soul.*

1. No permanent ego, only passing states of consciousness. (Compare this modern view with Buddhistic psychology.)
2. Spiritual ego theory. Lotze, "Microcosmus"; James, "Psychology," Vol. I.; Green, "Prolegomena to Ethics," Book I.; Dresser, "In Search of a Soul," Chaps. I., II., IX.
3. Creation theory. Soul disintegrates at death.
4. Reincarnation. Annie Besant. Walker. Vedantism.
5. Various theories of will, attention, and activity. James, "Briefer Psychology"; Stout, "Analytic Psychology," Vol. I.

F. *Place and Meaning of the Active Principle in Man.*
 1. Philosophically considered.
 2. Practical value as opposed to mere thought or the affirmation of ideals.

G. *The Higher Nature of Man.*
 I. Ethically considered.
 1. "All is good" criticised. The problem of evil.
 2. The responsibility of high ideals in reference to society and to religion. (See "Ethical Religion," W. M. Salter.)
 3. Meliorism as opposed to easy-going optimism.
 II. Spiritually considered.
 1. The inner self. Emerson's "Over-soul." Divine communion, receptivity, humility, the spiritual life, love, super-consciousness, intuition, the Christ.
 2. The law of spiritual development. "Seek first the kingdom." Poise. Meditation. Practical idealism.
 3. The ultimate value and meaning of suffering in relation to the spiritual life and the divine ideal.

H. *Philosophical Problems suggested by the Existence of a Higher Nature or Active Spiritual Principle in Man.*
 1. Pantheism.
 2. Fatalism.
 3. Pessimism.
 4. The relation of these three inadequate views to the Vedanta philosophy.

5. Theory of the divine immanence. Is it wholly plausible?

6. Freedom and the place and meaning of ethical selves.

7. Comparison of theories of reality.

(*a*) Phenomenalism. John Stuart Mill.

(*b*) Reality "unknowable." Kant and Spencer criticised.

(*c*) Mysticism, Oriental systems, Neo-Platonism, Schopenhauer, Deussen's "Elements of Metaphysics."

(*d*) Reality considered as the ground and owner of all appearances. Hegel, Bradley ("Appearance and Reality"), works of Professor Royce.

(*e*) Eclectic empiricism. Reality what it shall prove itself to be. James, "The Will to Believe"; Dresser, "Voices of Hope," chapter on "The Progressing God"; *International Journal of Ethics*, July, 1898, "The Activity-Experience."

NOTE.— The author will be glad to receive communications concerning this outline of study, or add to the very inadequate list of references. Comments on the theory of "The Progressing God" as the conception of reality which best fits the facts of evolution and of our moral consciousness are particularly desired.

APPENDIX B.

TOPICAL SYLLABUS (ISSUED BY CLARK UNIVERSITY) TO AID IN THE SCIENTIFIC STUDY OF THE PSYCHOLOGY OF HEALTH AND DISEASE.

If you have had any experience or know of others who have had in the line of disease cured or prevented by prayer, teachings of Christian science, hypnotism, or any form of mental treatment, kindly contribute an account of such cases. If you have tried or know of others who have tried any of these *without success*, please report these also, and as fully as possible.

This information is sought solely for the purpose of making a scientific study of the relation of states of mind to the conditions of bodily well-being, and will not be used for any other purpose.

Write your account in your own way. The following topics are given simply as a guide. Do not follow them unless it is easier to do so.

Your communication will be confidential if you wish it so. Names are never used in any case.

Please give a few words about the temperament,

also give the age, nationality, occupation, and church affiliations of each person reported.

Please send *at least one* record.

A. *The Disease.*

Hereditary; contagious; result of fear; from study; from worry. Duration. Age when it began. Previous treatments. Names and addresses (when practicable) of two or more physicians who treated the case. Time elapsing between last treatment with medicine and beginning of mental treatment.

B. *The Treatment.*

Duration. Method. (Verbal suggestion, telepathic, silent treatment, absent treatment, self-healing, etc.) If reporting your own case, mention any special feeling, thought, hope, fear, or expectation while being treated.

In a case of "self-healing" tell how you came to believe that you could heal yourself. Mention any books or teachers that were helpful. What was your method of treating yourself?

In cases of "absent treatment" was this method as satisfactory in its results as other methods? In such cases were you aware of the exact time when you were to be treated? In "silent treatment" what instructions or explanations were given at first treatment? How was your mind usually occupied during the treatment?

C. *The Cure.*

When, in the course of the treatment, improvement began to be noticed. Rapid or slow. Permanent or relapsing. Time that has elapsed since cure. Time required for the cure. Strongest evidence of cure. Any other effects of the teaching or of the treatment on (your) life.

D. *Unsuccessful Treatment.*

If treatment was unsuccessful, please report "A" and "B" as before. Also give facts that may account for the failure. Report "E" as fully as possible.

E. *Literature, etc.*

Please mention any literature bearing upon the subject, and make a brief statement of any views you may hold and be willing to express. What (if anything) in your school education bore upon this subject or later became a help to you in understanding the teaching? Do you think anything could be introduced into the schools that would be valuable on this line? Where were you educated? Was psychology studied? Age of leaving school. Quantity and kind of reading since school life ended. Effect upon (your) life.

Kindly send returns to

HORATIO W. DRESSER.

THE ARENA CO., BOSTON, MASS.

www.ingramcontent.com/pod-product-compliance
Lightning Source LLC
Chambersburg PA
CBHW020156170426
43199CB00010B/1071